Are You Respectful Today?

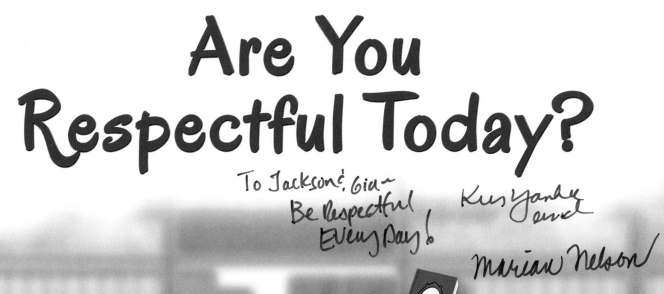

To Jackson & Gia~
Be Respectful
Every Day!

Kris Yankee
and
Marian Nelson

FERNE PRESS

Written by Kris Yankee and Marian Nelson • Illustrated by Jeff Covieo

Are You Respectful Today?
Becoming a Better You! series

Layout and cover design by Jacqueline L. Challiss Hill
Illustrations by Jeff Covieo
Illustrations created with digital graphics

Printed in Canada

Summary: Kids learn ways to be respectful toward themselves and others.
Library of Congress Cataloging-in-Publication Data
Yankee, Kris and Nelson, Marian
Are You Respectful Today?/Kris Yankee and Marian Nelson–First Edition
ISBN-13: 978-1-938326-25-7
1. Respect. 2. Self-esteem. 3. Character education. 4. Confidence.
I. Yankee, Kris and Nelson, Marian II. Title
Library of Congress Control Number: 2014938280

FERNE PRESS

Ferne Press is an imprint of Nelson Publishing & Marketing
366 Welch Road, Northville, MI 48167
www.nelsonpublishingandmarketing.com
(248) 735-0418

More Praise for *Are You Respectful Today?*

"I am currently integrating Book 1 *Are You Confident Today?* into an upcoming middle school retreat. Now, I have another powerful tool for my arsenal in reaching out to this age group. Being respectful is always relevant, timeless, and a spot-on reminder for all ages. Nicely done!"

~Tim Flaherty, Middle School Youth Minister

"Being a mom of two boys, I always want to make sure that I am giving them the tools they need to become caring, loving, and respectful young boys and men. *Are You Respectful Today?* is positive and fun, while sharing creative ideas to help our children be the best they can be! Loved the illustrations!"

~Kari Rhea, Mother of two boys, PTO President

Dedication

This book is dedicated to all of the great role models, parents, educators, and individuals who are committed to building healthy character in people of all ages. It is because of your loyalty to humanity that we will see the lasting results in our children. They will grow up to be positive role models for the next generation.

A special thank you to the staff at Nelson Publishing & Marketing, Patti Grover, Kathy Dyer, Amanda Clothier, and Jacqueline Hill, for their ideas, suggestions, support, and vision for the future.

Every day is a new day.

Today is about being respectful.

When you are respectful, you're considerate and polite.
You can show respect by caring about yourself and others.

Try this! Each day when you wake up, say out loud,

"I'm going to be kind to everyone."

Your dad may help you get your lunch ready or check your homework.
It's important to him to make sure you're ready for school.
You look up to your dad which shows you respect him.

"Thanks, Dad!"

Your sister shows respect for you by listening to you sing a song you learned at school.

By playing carefully with your cousin's toys, you show respect for her.

Hey! You're smart and know how to be respectful in school.

Listening quietly while you learn the lesson from your teacher shows you appreciate and respect her.

You can be respectful of your classmates
by using a quiet voice during library time.

When you're having fun,
waiting for your turn can be difficult.

Being patient shows respect for others.

Your coach or leader will know you are respectful when you listen and pay attention to details.

Planting by

High 5

"We Grow Character."

Look at yourself in the mirror every day and say,
"I'm a kind and caring person. I'm helpful and I want to make the
world a better place." Positive thoughts lead to healthy thinking.

To be healthy, you need to respect your body.
Make careful choices about the kinds of foods you eat and what you
drink. Exercise and eating right keep you alert and focused.

Sometimes we forget to be respectful.
You might say something rude to your friend, brother, or sister.
Be sure to apologize for acting that way and
make sure it doesn't happen again.

"I'm really sorry."

Show your grandparents that you appreciate them by treating them respectfully. Always look for the good in each other.

You can show respect by helping your neighbor
you don't know very well.

Every time you go to a friend's soccer game or
your sister's dance recital, you're being respectful of them.

Great job!

If you treat others with respect, most times they'll treat you the same. To get respect, you have to give respect. It's easy! When everyone takes responsibility for their own behavior, we are respectful people.

We need to be respectful of our environment and other people's property.
Don't litter, always recycle,
and be careful with items that don't belong to you.

Judging people who are different than us is very disrespectful.

Be very considerate of others' differences.
Look for the things that make you
alike rather than different.

Decide to start today. Acknowledge your talents and abilities.
Practice becoming a better YOU!

What I'm good at...	Strengths	Work on
Sharing with sister	★	
Patience on the playground	★	
Studying spelling		😐
Following directions	★	
Exercising	★	
How I treat others		😐
Cleaning up the environment	★	
Eating healthy foods		😐

Why do we need to be respectful?
When you are respectful, you will

- be a better listener
- show more kindness
- be patient
- be tolerant and understand others' differences
- take care of your body by eating healthy foods
- exercise regularly

Now you know why respect is important.
Life is happier and more fulfilling with a respectful heart.

When you lay your head down on your pillow tonight, remind yourself of all the ways you showed respect for yourself and others.

Remember that being respectful takes practice.

Practice, practice, and never give up. Give yourself a big hug!

Reflections

- Have you ever met someone who seemed very different than you, but then you realized you had a lot in common?
- What are your healthy eating and exercising goals? Have you ever thought of starting a walking club in your neighborhood or at school?
- What would happen if you focused only on the things you didn't like about someone else? Would you be friends with that person?
- Name four things in our environment that we need to care for. Choose one and write about how we can preserve it.
- Compare and contrast the best ways we are preserving our water and trees.
- Why is it important to apologize and make sure the hurt you caused doesn't happen again?
- Discuss how being confident makes you a more respectful person.
- Why is it hard to trust someone who is repeatedly rude to you?
- Name ten positive qualities about yourself and ten about your best friend. What differences do you see between the two lists?
- How do you show respect to older people?
- Name two times an older person taught you something new.
- How can you practice being patient?
- How should you treat other people's belongings? Why is it important to be careful with others' belongings?
- How can you use words to show respect?
- What would it be like if everyone showed respectful behavior?

Tips for Creating Respectful Kids

- Encourage kids to set five healthy eating goals and five exercise goals. Have them track their progress daily.
- Have kids practice positive self-talk first thing in the morning, such as, "Today's a great day!"
- When meeting someone new, encourage kids to focus on their similarities and not their differences. Have them count how many things each of them have in common with the other.
- Older generations are wiser than younger ones. Teach kids to see the value of older people's wisdom.
- Instill in kids the habit of using positive words toward family members.
- Provide opportunities that teach kids patience, such as waiting and taking turns.
- Set a good example of being respectful toward others by being prepared, organized, and on time for appointments.
- Discuss with your child why respectful body language is important. Be sure to provide examples of positive and negative body language postures.

Dear Reader,

Like confidence, respect is learned at a young age. Without respect, kids plow through life focusing on the differences between themselves and others. They can be hurtful and may do lasting damage to another person. Even though we are unique individuals, the things we have in common far outweigh our differences.

Why raise respectful kids? It's simple: respect breeds appreciation. An appreciative person does not complain but looks for the positive aspects in life.

Families and schools around the globe are instituting programs that develop respectful characteristics in children. *Are You Respectful Today?* is a great tool to use in addition to any character program or to support family goals.

We believe the world is a better place with people who are respectful. Wouldn't you agree?

Kris Yankee and Marian Nelson

Author Biographies

Photo by Eric Yankee

Kris Yankee is a freelance editor, writer, wife, and mom. Kris feels blessed to have been able to be a part of this new series, as she believes that the values presented are those that she hopes to instill in her own children. She is an award-winning author of *Are You Confident Today?* co-written with Marian Nelson, *Cracking the Code: Spreading Rumors,* and *Tommy Starts Something Big: Giving Cuddles with Kindness,* co-written with Chuck Gaidica. For more information about Kris, please visit her at facebook.com/BooksbyKrisYankee.

For the last nine years, Marian Nelson has been the publisher for Nelson Publishing & Marketing. She is happy to launch this new series of books called **Becoming a Better You!** Helping people grow to become better individuals has been her life passion. Formerly an educator for nearly twenty years, Marian keeps her focus on the children of the world, actively pursuing concepts of building healthy character. She continues to reach out to as many as possible in her talks and books. It is her hope that people will focus on learning and growing from the concepts presented in this book series and to work on self-improvement.

Photo by Eric Yankee

Visit us at nelsonpublishingandmarketing.com • parentsforcharacter.blogspot.com • facebook.com/pages/Nelson-Publishing-Marketing

Illustrator Biography

Jeff Covieo has been drawing since he could hold a pencil and hasn't stopped since. He has a BFA in photography from College for Creative Studies in Michigan and works in the commercial photography field, though drawing and illustration have been his avocation for years. *Are You Respectful Today?* is the ninth book he has illustrated.